SHOSTAKOVICH

SONATA

in D minor, Opus 40

FOR CELLO AND PIANO

(LEONARD ROSE)

Published in 2019 by Allegro Editions

Sonata for Cello and Piano
ISBN: 978-1-9748-9972-2 (paperback)

Cover design by Kaitlyn Whitaker

Cover image: "Cello" by Mindscape Studio, courtesy of Shutterstock;
"Black and White Piano Keys" by Nerthuz, courtesy of iStock;
"Music Sheet" by danielo, courtesy of Shutterstock

ALLEGRO EDITIONS

SONATA
in D minor, Opus 40
for Cello and Piano

I.

Edited by LEONARD ROSE

DMITRI SHOSTAKOVICH
(1906-1975)

II.

III.

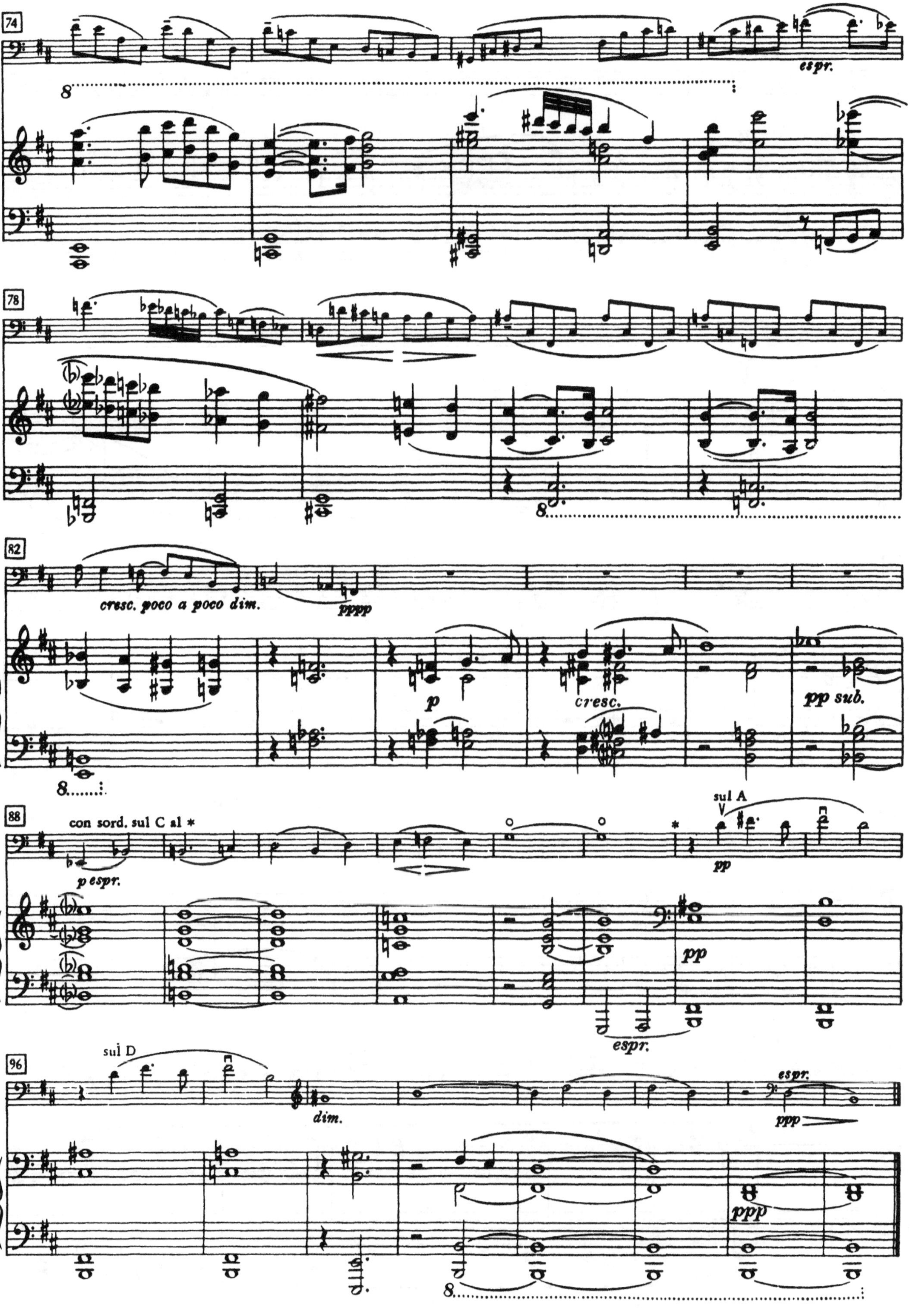
74
espr.
78
82
cresc. poco a poco dim.
pppp
p
cresc.
pp sub.
88
con sord. sul C al *
p espr.
sul A
pp
pp
espr.
96
sul D
dim.
espr.
ppp
ppp

IV.

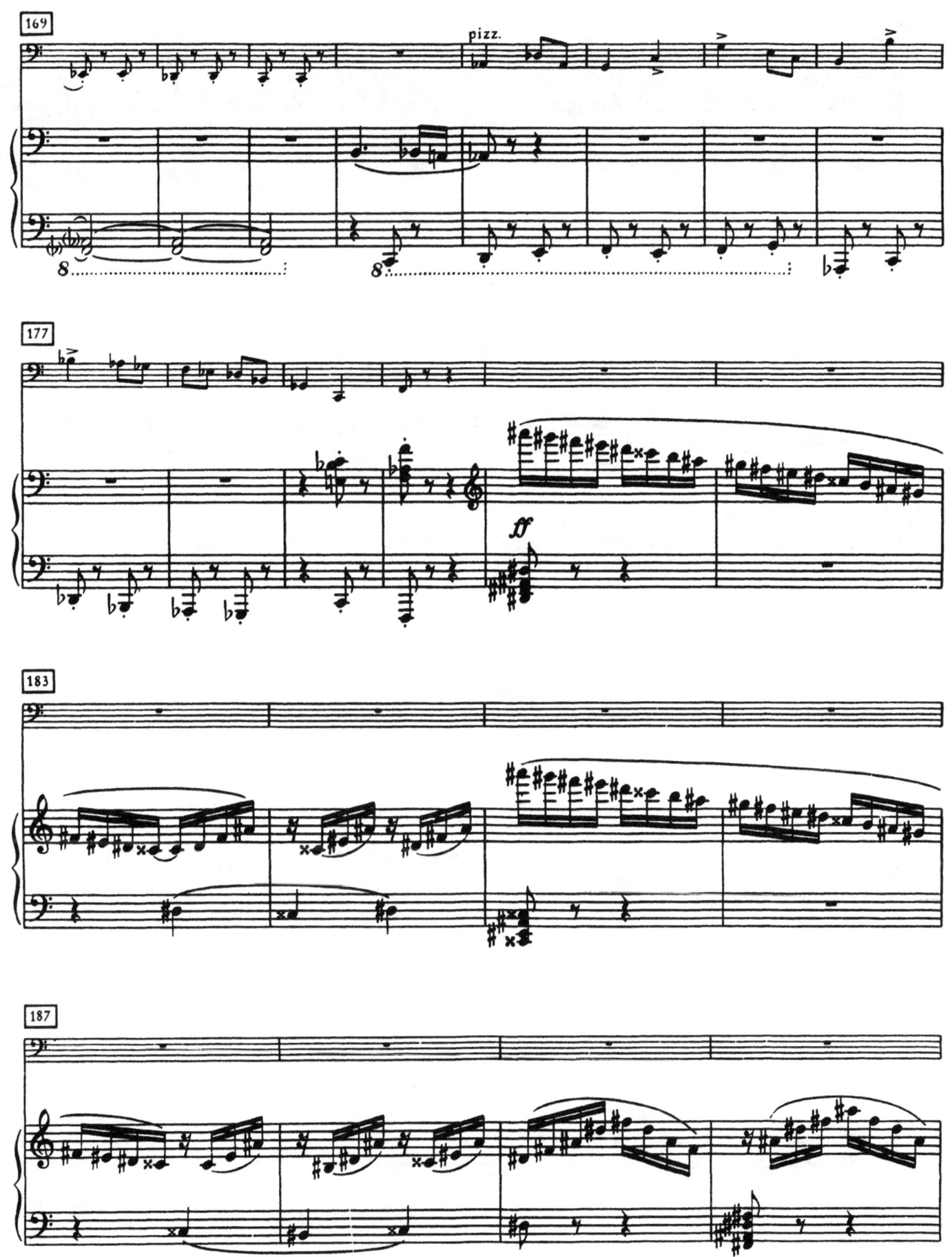

SONATA
in D minor, Opus 40
for Cello and Piano

CELLO

I.

Edited by LEONARD ROSE

Allegro ma non troppo (♩ = 138)

DMITRI SHOSTAKOVICH
(1906-1975)

CELLO

CELLO

CELLO

III.

CELLO

www.ingramcontent.com/pod-product-compliance
Lightning Source LLC
LaVergne TN
LVHW061344060426
835512LV00016B/2661